D0980145

AN INTRODUCTION TO
A Course in Miracles

AN INTRODUCTION TO
A Course in Miracles

◆   MIRACLE DISTRIBUTION CENTER   ◆

Written for Miracle Distribution Center by Robert Perry

Cover and book design: Steve Doolittle

See page 53 for information on how to obtain additional copies of this book.

Printed in the United States of America.

ISBN 0-9618309-0-5

TABLE OF CONTENTS

PREFACE

A Course in Miracles is a 1200 page, three volume book. It is also a phenomenon, a work whose content and characteristics, whose history and impact on the world are so unique that there are no neat labels or categories for it. The Course was authored not by a person, but by an "inner voice" that dictated the material to a research psychologist in the midst of a remarkable, unfolding story beginning in the mid-1960's. Its teaching, again falling outside of preexisting molds, combines the insights of contemporary psychology, with the spiritual wisdom of the East, and much of the essence of Christianity. The Course, however, is more than an abstract philosophy and includes a highly specific training program in the practical application of its principles, focusing on forgiveness in the area of relationships.

In our mundane, physical world and in a secular age that appears to have forgotten God, *A Course in Miracles* is seemingly itself a miracle—a breakthrough of God into the world. In its story, its teaching and its results, it speaks of another reality, one that lies beyond our everyday experience. The Course certainly has been a "miracle" in the lives of thousands of people who are students of it, showing a profound ability for facilitating deep inner transformation. In fact, a whole spontaneous movement has grown up around it since its publication in 1976. Yet because the Course is such a singular phenomenon, there being no ready-made mental slots to file it in, and because it is large and often difficult to grasp, this book has been created to answer the need for a clear, concise overview.

WHAT IS
A Course in Miracles?

The purpose of *A Course in Miracles* is to be an agent of healing, inner healing. As a consummate physician, the Course both diagnoses the problem and combines wisdom, beauty, logic and compassion into a remedy that is at once simple, practical, and extremely effective.

In a world pervaded by pain and suffering, there seems to be a limitless number of problems, of all kinds and on all levels. This locks us into an endless, frantic juggling act of trying to keep our lives from being swallowed up by the difficulties that face us on all fronts. The Course seeks to cut through this bewildering complexity right to the core, to the central problem of human existence, and to there lay its gentle remedy. All problems, it says, are really one problem. From the external tragedies of war, famine, disease and death; to the deeper, inner crises of loneliness, emptiness and despair, to the cosmic spiritual dilemma of separation from God, they are all the same. "One problem, one solution. Salvation is accomplished."[1]

The Course is thus an exercise in ultimate practicality—"...it is the practical with which this course is most concerned"[2]—for by identifying and alleviating this one problem it seeks to bring healing to every level of our lives. What is this problem? According to the Course it is an inner malady that lies deep within us. It is not an unfair conflict between ourselves and outside forces. It is a conflict in our own mind, between our freely chosen beliefs and our own best interests. *A Course in Miracles* is therefore "...a course in mind training,"[3] teaching us to make the choices that will heal this inner conflict and bring instead inner peace.

The Course is certainly not the only useful guide in this respect. It states that it is only one form "...of the universal course. There are many thousands of other forms, all with the same outcome."[4] The Course is universal, not sectarian, in its themes. In fact, it expresses itself using the forms, ideas and terminology of some of the greatest and most influential attempts to improve the human condition. Taking a look at the ways in which the Course does this can tell us a great deal about what it is.

EDUCATION

Much of the basic structure of the Course is modelled after modern education, certainly one of the more influential attempts to improve our lot. As its title implies, it is designed as a "course," with three volumes: a text, setting forth the theoretical system; a workbook for students, containing 365 daily lessons; and a manual for teachers, based on the premise that, "To teach is to demonstrate."[5]

Like education, the goal of the Course is "learning," to train our minds in the acquisition of new concepts and perceptions. However, unlike normal education, the Course is not interested in teaching superficial knowledge and facts, but aims instead at a radical transformation of the fundamental mind-set through which we approach life, our basic stance or posture towards life. This stance is composed of our actual beliefs—very different from those we consciously hold—of what we are, what others are, what God is. Education on this level is clearly reeducation which demands, first of all, unlearning. "To learn this course requires willingness to question every value that you hold."[6]

We can glimpse the true nature of the Course's educational intent in the structure of its three volumes. The Text explains the concepts, but since the purpose of the Course is to go beyond an intellectual grasp to a full internalization of its principles, the Workbook for Students is included. Its brilliantly organized and highly structured one-year program is designed to begin a process of profound inner transformation, through which one becomes a "teacher," a living demonstration of the Course's principles. Issues associated with being such an example are then addressed in the Manual for Teachers.

PSYCHOLOGY

Another important attempt at healing the human condition has been modern psychology, with which the Course has important similarities. The approach of the Course is, in fact, very psychological. Because it sees all human ills as rooted in mental

4

illness, it sees all solutions as lying in mental healing. The practice of *A Course in Miracles* is therefore a kind of psychotherapy, in which the patient is ourselves and the therapist is our inner Teacher, or what the Course calls the Holy Spirit.

Furthermore, the Course has significant parallels with Freudian psychology. Both see man's conscious mind as floating on an ocean of unconsciousness. These deeper regions of mind are filled with tumultuous forces, churning with buried pain and hidden motives. As a result, both share a pessimistic view of man's present personality. In great contrast with Freud, however, the Course sees the possibility, in fact the certainty, of the transformation of that personality, by identifying an even deeper dimension of our makeup. Beneath our unconscious mind, says the Course, lies a transcendental, spiritual dimension, and this is our true nature. The purpose of the Course, then, is nothing less than the discovery of who we are. "...this course was sent to open up the path of light to us, and teach us, step by step, how to return to the eternal Self we thought we lost."[7]

EASTERN RELIGION

Some of the deepest and most penetrating insights into the human condition have come from the East, especially the religions of Hinduism and Buddhism. There, for thousands of years, sages have sought liberation from suffering and direct contact with reality through ascending the heights of their own consciousness. We in the West are only now learning some of the importance of their insights.

It could be said that in many ways the Course adopts an Eastern picture of both this world and of true reality. Their commonalities might be stated thusly:

> — This world we live in, this massive panorama of innumerable separate bodies, all moving through separate places and separate times, this world of suffering, of disease, old age and death is an illusion. It is not reality at all but only a dream.

> —Reality is a oneness which transcends distinctions, differences, and change, a condition that is outside space and time, and beyond comprehension as we know it. The Course calls this "Heaven," and it is this condition that we truly are.

—The goal of life, then, is not focused in this world, on amassing worldly power, fortune, or pleasure. Our goal is to wake up, to realize who we really are, to unloose our attachments to this world and awaken into unlimited bliss.

CHRISTIANITY

Without question the religion of Christianity and the figure of Jesus Christ have been the most powerful influences in the last 2000 years of civilization. It is perhaps because of this influence, and because of the great significance the Course accords Jesus, that the Course's most obvious ties are with Christianity. In fact, one of the Course's more startling claims is that it was authored, through inner dictation, by the author of Christianity, Jesus Christ. Echoing the Bible, it thus presents the image of a contemporary revealed scripture, a modern-day message from God to mankind.

As one might expect, the Course has many deep similarities with traditional Christianity, similarities which would also perhaps comprise its main differences with the major themes of Eastern religion. Both the Course and Christianity see the root cause of our predicament as embodied in the idea of sin, in our capacity to break off relationship with God and others, and to attack instead of love. And both see the dynamic behind salvation as one of God's Spirit lovingly reaching down into the world and into our hearts, and then inspiring us to reach out to others in love and service; drawing us into relationship, relationship with other people and with the Divine.

The Course, however, is clearly intended not as a restatement, but as a purification, of traditional Christianity. It implies that by labelling sin and evil, and time and space ultimately real, Christianity has subtly added to our burden of guilt, reinforced our limitations and made God a punisher, instead of a lover. Of these ideas, the Course says, "This is not the Gospel I intended to offer you."[8] In its system, the key to our release is the fact that both our condition and its cornerstone, sin, are somehow dreams. Only what God wills is real and God wills only limitless love.

The Course's function as a purifier of Christianity is most easily seen in its use of Christian terminology. Many of the Course's primary terms are drawn from Christianity, but changed to reflect a purified and more universal perspective. A good example is the term "miracle," in which the Course reinterprets the traditional meaning of the word into psychological terms. Instead of a divine intervention in the physical world which heals the body, a "miracle" is a divine intervention in our minds which heals our thought-patterns.

* * *

The Course takes the insights from these rich traditions, along with many original ideas, and fuses them together into a completely original system, a perfectly unified microcosm, with its own terminology and imagery, its own logic and styles of thought, its own unique vision of reality and approach to the human condition. This system is relentlessly logical, being constructed with the tight, exacting reason of a geometric form, yet is infused with great literary artistry and poetic beauty. It is anchored in the loftiest of philosophical abstractions, yet is focused solely on penetrating and transforming the fabric of our everyday lives, the private intricacies of mind and heart. It is utterly uncompromising yet filled with a spirit of total freedom. It reasonably, beautifully and compellingly presents a totally radical and deeply challenging alternative to our basic approach to life.

The purpose of this system, and the reason it is designed to be a world unto itself, is to draw our minds into a completely different way of thinking. In this system, inner values relating to God, love, forgiveness and sharing—values that inspire us but seem impractical—become suddenly logical and natural. It is here we find much of the Course's amazing ability to transform minds.

Furthermore, because the primary thrust of the Course is to heal, not to explain or entertain, it possesses an extreme simplicity of focus. *"The course is simple. It has one function and one goal."*[9] For this reason it completely ignores most of the concerns we consider essential in life. It does not deal with far-flung theoretical issues, nor with science, history, economics, medicine, etc. Nor does the Course acknowledge individual differences, not even gender distinctions. In short, it leaves no room for our remarkable ability to get sidetracked. Instead, it presents a radical simplification of life's paramount issues, focusing all its energies on the single, crucial choice that can solve all of our problems.

What is this choice? It is the choice to heal the deep inner illness that is the source of our pain. The Course says that we are almost all unconsciously ruled by a mind-set of extreme separateness and attack, a condition of mental isolation in which we look upon the world through condemning eyes of judgment and anger. This mentality not only throws us into a state of war with the world, it also places us at war with ourselves, crippling us with guilt and walling us off in icy loneliness out of fear of the world around us.

To heal this mind-set we must realize that it is this, and not the world, that causes our pain. Furthermore, this mentality is not a true picture of reality. It is an illusion. Therefore, we can let go of condemnation and choose instead to see the light of Heaven in everyone and everything we look upon, reaching out to the world in a new relationship, one based on love, joining and giving. Healing our relationship with the world also heals our relationship with ourselves. We become innocent, peaceful and joyously happy.

We learn this critical lesson in the context of our everyday lives. This fact brings out another quality of the Course, its "down to earth" approach. As it says, "God takes you where you are and welcomes you."[10] The Course does not concentrate on articles of religious belief nor advocate withdrawal from the world. Its goal is not otherworldliness, but a practical, inner change in the arena of day-to-day living, which will make us happier, healthier people who are healing influences on the world around us.

This leads to the Course's heavy emphasis on human relationships, for it is in our perception of other people that our most important choices occur. It is here, in the area of relationships, that the Course perhaps most fully establishes its own distinctive path. "Time has been saved for you because you and your brother are together. This is the special means this course is using..."[11] A *Course in Miracles* could be called a course in the healing of relationships, for it is in how we see others that we can both get in touch with, and transcend, the ego-centeredness that is our fundamental problem. It is for this reason that forgiveness is the Course's central teaching, since forgiveness is the relinquishing of attack upon others in favor of love. In the choice to forgive we shine healing light deep into the hidden core of our brother's pain and our own, releasing us both as one into the reality of love.

We can now gain some idea of how the Course weaves together its diverse elements. It takes the essentially Eastern distinction between reality and illusion and applies it to the psychological level, saying that it is only our psychological illusions that block us from heavenly awareness. We then learn to undo these blocks in the context of the Christian emphasis on relationship; as an instrument and child of God and as a brother and healer to other people.

This synthesis can also help us understand the Course's strange title. The title *A Course in Miracles* means that its purpose is to train us in the eliciting of miracles, to educate us in the choice between the spiritual reality of love and oneness and the worldly illusion of attack and separateness, a choice that allows God's Spirit to heal both our brother's mind and our own. This healing then radiates outward, awakening a greater happiness, peace and joy in all living things.

Overall, *A Course in Miracles* presents the image of a modern holy book, sent as a healer of the core sickness of mankind. Its author uses his powers as a master educator, psychologist, sage and savior to create a rich and complex system totally concentrated on effecting the one, simple, inner change that can unleash all the rest. It says that the key to healing the human condition is within our grasp, within our own hearts and minds. In the choice to forgive, we can escape all the pain and suffering of the world, we can bring healing to the hearts of others and we can be reunited with God.

A Course in Miracles

The story behind how *A Course in Miracles* came to be written and published is an inspiring testimony to the teaching of the Course itself. As has been mentioned, the Course was not written in a conventional manner and the significance of its story is to be found in the overwhelming appearance that the same Voice that was dictating the words of the Course to its human "scribe," was also directing the entire situation, subtly orchestrating people and events into a complex drama with a meaning. The main character, then, of the Course's play is not the human players at all, but the author. For though he is never seen, he is the presence pointed to by all the events. As such, the story of the Course is a classic, timeless drama which echoes the great stories of the Bible. Like those stories, it is the power of God that is testified to, not that of His human instruments, which are usually fearful and confused, and even reluctant and rebellious. Those in the Course's story were all of these things. They were two agnostic, even atheistic, psychology professors, deeply immersed in the values of this world and full of conflict, both internal and interpersonal. But they joined together and gave the Holy Spirit the "little willingness" He requires and so became His instruments. And herein lies the meaning of the story of *A Course in Miracles*.

In 1965, Helen Schucman, 56, and Bill Thetford, 42, were colleagues in the Psychology Department of the Presbyterian Hospital at Columbia University's College of Physicians and Surgeons. Bill had hired Helen, shortly after becoming the director of the department in 1957, and both of them had found their jobs there to be extremely frustrating. Typical of a university setting, their department was filled with hostility, resentment and competition. This state of conflict extended past their department and included relationships with other departments and even other medical centers. To make matters worse, Helen and Bill's relationship, though essentially a cooperative one, was also ridden with stress and anger.

It was this state of affairs that finally prompted a very uncharacteristic and highly significant occurrence between them. One day in mid-1965, before a regular meeting, Bill made a lengthy and, for him, impassioned speech. "There must be a better way," he said—a better way of dealing with these meetings, with their professional relationships, and indeed their lives—"and I'm determined to find it." Their old way had brought nothing but strife and so he suggested a new approach, based on an attitude of acceptance and cooperation and a strategy of emphasizing the good.

This outburst was extremely out of character, and so was Helen's response. Unexpectedly, she exclaimed to Bill that he was right and that she would join with him in finding this better way.

This moment of joining represented an unprecedented turning point in their relationship. It was an example of what the Course calls a "holy instant," that moment we lay aside our characteristic patterns of thinking and feeling, which have failed us, and open ourselves to receive the truth, to receive "a better way." In this holy instant they established a "holy relationship," a transformation of the hidden foundation of their old relationship into a new one, based on a joint dedication to finding truth together. The holy instant and the holy relationship were implicit invitations to the Holy Spirit to enter their lives and their relationship and give the gift of healing that had been asked for.[12] It did not matter that Bill was agnostic and Helen a self-professed "militant atheist," for as long as two people "join in sharing one goal,"

> *God [through the Holy Spirit] will enter into their*
> *relationship, because He has been invited to come*
> *in...what difference does it make how the invita-*
> *tion is written? Does the paper matter, or the ink,*
> *or the pen?...If any two are joined, He must be*
> *there.*[13]

Far beyond what they had expected, this event was the catalyst which set in motion what was to affect the rest of their lives, and the lives of many others as well. The initial results took the form of three months of startling visionary and psychic experiences for Helen. She began to experience vivid mental images, both waking and sleeping. These formed into several long, gradually unfolding series that were symbolically rich and extremely emotionally involving. In the fact of their occurrence and the content of their themes, they seemed to be a sign that a critical beginning point had been reached, one that stood at the center of a long line and recalled to awareness the distant past in preparation for a new future.

The imagery experiences had many themes, but perhaps the most important images centered on a large black book. It was shown variously, in an ancient treasure chest and in a stork's pouch, with a string of pearls around it, a gold cross on it or the word "Aesculapius"—the Greek god of healing—written on it. In one vision she was told by an inner Voice, "This is your book." Yet neither she nor Bill had any idea what the book was until much later.

Helen also went through what she termed her "magic" phase. She began to have a series of remarkable psychic experiences and demonstrated a very great gift for knowing things she could not possibly have known through normal means. This, like her imagery experiences, caused her extreme inner turmoil, for she did not believe in the validity of such things. Yet she also had feelings of pride and self-inflation and so, appropriately, this whole period ended with a choice between her temptation to seeking power through her ability and her allegiance to Something higher, which could use her ability for good.

My own "magic" phase ended abruptly with a particularly clear picture episode in which I knew I had made an irrevocable choice. I saw myself entering a cave cut into a rock formation on a bleak wind-swept seacoast. All I found in the cave was a large and very old parchment scroll. Its ends were attached to heavy gold-tipped poles, and the scroll was wrapped around them so that they met in the middle of the scroll and were tied tightly together. With some difficulty I managed to untie the ends and open the scroll just enough to reveal the center panel, on which two words were written: "GOD IS." Then I un-

rolled the scroll all the way. As I did so, tiny letters began to appear on both sides of the panel. The silent Voice which I had "heard" before explained the situation mentally to me:

"If you look at the left side, you will be able to read the past," said the Voice. "If you look at the right side, you will be able to read the future."

The little letters on the sides of the panel were becoming clearer, but I hesitated only a moment before rolling up the scroll sufficiently to conceal everything except the center panel.

"I'm not interested in reading the past or the future, I said with finality. "I'll just stop with this."

The Voice sounded both reassured and reassuring.

"You made it that time," it said "Thank you."

And that, it seemed, was that.[14]

With this experience a strange, obscure process of preparation seemed to have concluded. Helen told Bill that she felt she was about to do something very unusual, yet neither she nor Bill had any notion of what that was to be. Then one night in October of that year, it happened. She telephoned Bill in a panic and told him that the now familiar inner Voice would not leave her alone. "It keeps saying, 'This is a course in miracles. Please take notes.' What am I going to do?" Being a psychologist, she feared for her sanity. Bill tried to calm and reassure her. He suggested that she do what it says, that she take the notes down in her customary shorthand. They could meet early at the office the next morning and if it did not make any sense, they would simply tear it up. At length she agreed, and sat down to record these words:

This is a course in miracles. It is a required course. Only the time you take it is voluntary. Free will does not mean that you can establish the curriculum. It means only that you can elect what you want to take at a given time. The course does not aim at teaching the meaning of love, for that is beyond what can be taught. It does aim, however, at removing the blocks to the awareness of

love's presence, which is your natural inheritance.
The opposite of love is fear, but what is all en-
compassing can have no opposite.
This course can therefore be summed up very
simply in this way:
Nothing real can be threatened.
Nothing unreal exists.
Herein lies the peace of God."[15]

Thus began a seven-year process of listening, recording, and transcribing that resulted in *A Course in Miracles.* This was the answer to their request for a better way, a fact they both recognized. The Course is therefore a concrete, verbal record of what the Holy Spirit does in every relationship and every mind that asks Him in: He takes it by the hand and leads it on a course, away from the pain and turmoil of the past to the peace of God within.

Helen would receive dictation almost daily, and she and Bill would meet in Bill's office as time permitted, she reading her shorthand notes and he typing up what was said. The dictation was not a form of automatic writing and she was in no special, altered state. The Voice could be shut off at will as she conducted the business of her life, in which case it would simply pick up later, often in mid-sentence. However, if she refused to listen, which she frequently did, she would become very anxious and irritable and would have difficulty sleeping, until she answered the inner call and returned to the dictation.

Helen's inner ambivalence is one of the major themes of the story. On the one hand she was highly threatened by the spiritual content of the material and she resented the time taken up by the dictation. But on the other hand there seemed to be another Helen who took her function as scribe very seriously, for she displayed great care in accurately recording the words given her and she even came to consider the Course her life's work. "It seemed to be a special assignment I had somehow, somewhere agreed to complete."[16]

Helen's ambivalence toward the Course was at least partially rooted in her conflicting feelings about its author. She was convinced that the author was Jesus, as the Course itself claims, and on one level she seemed to have a very deep and intimate rela-

15

tionship with him. Yet, consciously, there was extreme fear and resentment concerning Jesus. This may have related to the fact that as a child she sought very diligently for God yet never found Him, which seemed to have left a great void in her, filled with feelings of betrayal by Him.

Helen's emotional difficulty with the Course was one of the reasons that Bill was so essential to the whole process. Without his constant reassurance and support, it simply would not have been completed. As such, "It represented a truly collaborative venture..."[17] between the two of them. Their relationship was still often quite difficult, but in their work on the Course there was a true spirit of harmony and unity, as if a part of them understood the real significance of their collaboration. There was also a real dedication to fulfilling what they considered a sacred trust that had apparently been given them. Because of this the Course stands today as Helen heard it, virtually word for word, except for the omission of some personal material that came at the beginning.

The process of dictation was finally finished in September 1972. With this, a long chapter came to a close and it was time for the next player to come onto the scene. That same month Bill read an intriguing article entitled "Mysticism and Schizophrenia" by Kenneth Wapnick. Ken had been raised as a Jew, had received his Ph.D. in psychology, and was now eagerly pursuing a search for God in the context of Christian monasticism. Through a series of occurrences he was introduced to Helen and Bill only days before leaving on a trip to Israel, which he was taking after deciding to become a monk. When he returned to the United States six months later, it was only to tie up loose ends before leaving again for a more permanent stay in a monastery in Israel.

Yet he also had in mind to examine this book he had been told about. It was then that Helen showed him the manuscript of *A Course in Miracles*. He was overwhelmed and realized very quickly that it was the most profound and the most beautiful material he had ever encountered. The Course's perfect integration of psychology and religion brought together and fulfilled both his training as a psychologist and his desire for God, as if his whole life had been a preparation for this. He changed all his plans, deciding against being a monk. He moved to New York to be with Helen and Bill and dedicated his life to working with the Course.

Ken quickly became a close friend to both Bill and Helen and the three of them formed a kind of spiritual family in their work on, and practice of, the Course. Even though the dictation had been completed, there was still much work to be done on the Course in terms of capitalizing, punctuating, paragraphing and sectioning. Ken was extremely instrumental in this, feeling an intense inner drive to have this job completed, which finally occurred in early 1975.

But what were they to do now? Over the years the feeling had grown in Helen and Bill that even though the Course came in response to a personal request, the answer was not meant for them alone. Yet they did not think it was their place to be the ones making it available to others. Then one day in May, 1975, Bill attended a conference on Kirlian photography. The introductory lecture was given by a woman named Judith Skutch and as he sat in the audience, Bill felt an inner connection with her and a need to meet her.

That very night Judith Skutch went home and felt herself to be at the lowest point in her life. Although she was at the height of a busy and rewarding career in sponsoring research and networking individuals in the field of parapsychology, she felt devoid of meaning and purpose. A crucial, spiritual dimension was lacking and this was causing her great emotional and even physical pain. That night, alone in her bedroom, she found herself crying out, "Won't Someone up there please help me?"

Her answer, it seems, was not long in coming. A few days later a friend invited her to meet Bill Thetford and Helen Schucman for lunch. In the meantime she was told by a numerologist that within a year she would publish "one of the most important spiritual documents known to humanity."[18] When she met Bill and Helen they felt an immediate, innate rapport. The two of them told her their remarkable story and handed her the manuscript of *A Course in Miracles. As* she read the first words, a wave of gratitude washed over her, tears ran down her face and she knew that this was the answer to her prayer, this was her map home.

With the addition of Judy the many years of quiet preparation were over and it was time to "let the cat out of the bag." Judy seemed to have an endless number of friends and contacts, and so what had for years been locked in a closet, the "guilty secret" of two psychologists, now found itself circulating around the country in the form of hundreds of Xeroxed copies. The Course demonstrated an immediate and dramatic appeal, far beyond what Helen and Bill had ever imagined, instantly attracting scores of serious and devoted students. It seemed to have a life of its own, changing lives, inspiring the formation of groups, finding its way into foreign countries. Bill and Helen had never even considered publishing the material, yet now several publishers came forward asking to do just that. However, each time as the foursome met and listened within the answer was "no." They were finally told by the Voice that only those who had the Course as their focus and nothing else, were to publish it. Helen, Bill, Ken and Judy then realized it was their task to publish the Course and resolved to do so under the foundation that Judy and her husband had started for their work in parapsychology.

Their only problem was that they had no money. The next morning Judy received a call from a man in Mexico who had received a copy of the Course from a friend of Judy's and was now studying it with a group of people. "I am calling to tell you that I was guided to sell a piece of property recently, and with the proceeds I want to underwrite the first hardcover edition of five thousand sets of *A Course in Miracles*. It must be done properly and as soon as possible."[19] And so in June of 1976, after an utterly unique history, the Course became available in published form.

*   *   *

Thus was born out of the midst of a troubled relationship between two agnostic psychologists, from within a university in the middle of New York City—out of the very heart of modern, secular civilization—a voice for God in our times and a great force of healing in the world. In a world filled with pain, where a better way is so deeply needed, these two individuals asked for one, and through them an answer was given for all. In fact, one of the great themes of the story is the answering of the spiritual searches of everyone involved: Helen's childhood search for God, Bill's request for a better way, Ken's quest to live close to God and do His will, and Judy's cry, "Won't Someone up there please help me?"

Perhaps most striking of all is the fact that not only did the story behind the Course appear to be "authored" by something beyond the human realm—something that seemingly brought together and directed handpicked individuals along a logical progression according to a preconceived plan—but this "something" did so in a way that specifically reflected the teachings of *A Course in Miracles*. This creates the appearance that the author of the Course and the "author" of the events which produced it, were one and the same. The story can therefore be seen as a testimony to the Course's view of how the Holy Spirit and Jesus work in our lives. And the Course can be seen as a transcribed record of that work in the lives of two people.

In both the Course and its story we see the same scenario. No matter how immersed we are in a life of pain, frustration and aloneness, when we open our minds in a holy instant and reach out for something new, we will be answered. When we let down our defenses enough to join with another and to allow the Holy Spirit into our lives, a Light will be unleashed with the power to shine away all that stands between us and the peace of God. We will be given companions with whom to share holy relationships, and in whom to finally discover the true nature of the Light. And together with our companions we will form a window through which this Light can shine out to everyone, showing the entire world a better way.

A Course in Miracles

REALITY AND ILLUSION

Although the Course is extremely practical, its practicality is founded in a purely abstract view of the nature of reality. In summarizing the teaching of *A Course in Miracles,* it is with this abstract foundation that we must begin.

Beyond this world entirely, beyond anything physical, beyond time, space and form of any kind, lies what the Course calls **Heaven.** Heaven is a condition of such exaltation and immensity that it completely surpasses our present ability to describe, comprehend or imagine. We can, however, gain a sense of the direction in which it lies by describing Heaven with the ideas of oneness, peace, joy and love.

ONENESS: Heaven is pure oneness. There are no bodies, no different places, and no separate moments of time. There is only an infinite expanse of unified awareness. In Heaven our seemingly separate identities mingle and merge, uniting to form a single universal Self, which the Course calls **Christ.** Christ, in turn, reposes in a perfect intimate union with **God,** our Creator, the Lord of Heaven, the centerpole of existence. The Course's view of Heaven thus combines Eastern concepts of formlessness and oneness with Western ideas of companionship with, and worship of, God. "What is Heaven but a song of gratitude and love and praise by everything created to the Source of its creation?"[20]

PEACE AND JOY: Heaven is characterized by pure, unbridled happiness. Experiencing a profound, ecstatic rapture that fulfills and outstrips all possible want, we know perfect joy. In an infinite state, without disturbance or the passing of time, we are at peace.

LOVE: The idea that best combines all aspects of Heaven is love. Love is joyous union. In its true form, love is the holiness within ourselves rejoicing over and sharing itself with the holiness in another. Heaven, therefore, is the experience of perfect, boundless love, a joyous union with all that is.

In starkest contrast with this picture is our experience of life in this world. In fact, it is fundamental to the Course's system that Heaven and the **world** are complete opposites. This difference is so great that many of us cannot believe that a thing such as Heaven even exists. It is not hard to see why. For every characteristic of Heaven there is a corresponding and opposite characteristic of life in this world, the only life we now know.

SEPARATENESS: In the world, there is no such thing as true oneness. "Look at the world, and you will see nothing attached to anything beyond itself. All seeming entities can come a little nearer, or go a little farther off, but cannot join."[21] What we see is a lonely collection of separate minds trapped in separate bodies, moving through separate points in time. It is a picture of alienation, with each lonely fragment caught in an endless, frustrating, hopeless search for completion.

PAIN: This world is fraught with pain and suffering, the bodily pain of physical illness and deterioration, the emotional pains of anger, hate, guilt, insecurity, frustration and fear. All of them put together provide an underlying, all-pervading sense of unfulfillment, incompleteness, and lack that haunts and drains life from everything we experience.

SIN AND EVIL: We may not use these words, but we all carry an overpowering sense of something "bad" out there, something with the intent to hurt, something deserving of punishment. Anger and hatred are the emotions which tell us it is "out there." Guilt is the emotion which tells us it is within ourselves. Wherever we see it, we respond to it with **fear**. Fear, in fact, is the emotion that summarizes the essence of life in this world. Fear is a shrinking into separateness, a painful withdrawal from the sinfulness and guilt we see within everything. We now can most clearly see the contrast between Heaven and the world. Whereas the world is governed by fear, a painful recoil from sin, Heaven is ruled by the opposite dynamic of love, a joyous, expansive union with unlimited holiness.

Heaven and the world, then, are indeed complete opposites. One is the fulfillment of all that yearns within us; yet, unfortunately, we seem to be trapped in the other. In a way, every impasse in life is this one. We all want something better, we want to be happy, but we seem to be trapped by forces beyond our control. This is our central dilemma, a dilemma for which the Course has a radical answer. The world, it says, cannot trap us, limit us or control us, for the world is an illusion. It does not actually exist. It is a dream, and we are the ones, billions of years ago, who fell asleep and dreamed it up. Heaven is the only reality. Our true nature has never left Heaven and is there this very moment, completely unaware of the world. Heaven is now, and will always be, our home.

The implications of this are profound. If we have never really separated from God, we can return any time we choose. This is the liberating heart of the Course's message. There is nothing we need fight against and nothing we need pay for. We need only awaken to where we already are.

This thought strikes at the heart of all the obstacles we feel to happiness and love. What are these obstacles? One is certainly the world. It seems to be the world that stifles our fulfillment, surrounding us with opposing forces and with a thousand limiting circumstances. To gain anything we must fight against the massive web of obstacles, impediments and enemies that encircles us. And yet, if the world is our own dream, this battle is meaningless. Far from opposing our will, the world *does* our will. Therefore, we are completely free. If we are the dreamer, it is we who can make the dream a happy one, and it is we who can stop dreaming altogether and wake up whenever we want.

Another obstacle we feel is an inner one: our "inherent" limitation and sinfulness. And yet, this is a picture of us in the world, a picture that, like the world itself, is an illusion. According to the Course, we are still exactly as God created us, for we do not have the power to create ourselves. Our goal, then, is not to change ourselves, or even to "grow," it is simply to change our thinking and wake up to the unlimited, innocent Son of God that we already are.

Because we believe that we have sinned, we feel that before we can be happy, before we can be close to God, we must right the scales of justice and pay for what we have done. Yet this, too, is a dream. We do not need to appease an angry God by paying for our sins. We are not truly guilty, we just *feel* guilty. Man may believe he is black with sin, "but all the while his Father shines on him, and loves him with an everlasting Love which his pretenses cannot change at all."[22]

This single idea, then, that Heaven is reality and the world is illusion, sweeps away all of our obstacles to perfect happiness. It holds out to us the promise of complete deliverance. If the problem is not in reality but only in our mind, then all we need do is change our mind and we are free.

THE HOLY SPIRIT

Awakening to Heaven is not quite as easy as it sounds, however. The Course says that each one of us has been dreaming the dream of the world for millions of years. As a result, the "reality" of the world, with all its laws and all its ways, has penetrated so deeply into our minds that it holds a viselike grip on level after level of our subconscious. Heaven has been completely blotted from our awareness. Letting go of the world seems to be a horrifying leap into nothingness.

Therefore, since *we* could not bridge the gulf between reality and our illusion, God extended a part of Himself into the dream, to lead us out of the hell we made back to Heaven. This is the **Holy Spirit,** God's Voice in this world, the Father's Answer to His children's nightmare. In the form of the Holy Spirit, God is with us as an active, guiding, healing Presence. The function of the Holy Spirit is to answer the deepest and only need we have within the dream: the healing of our minds. His task, therefore, is a kind of divine psychotherapy on a global and universal scale. He is a Presence that pervades the unconscious level of all living minds, ceaselessly engaging in a one-to-one, deep-level dialogue with every frightened mind in need of healing.

The Holy Spirit represents one of the Course's central themes: We cannot make it alone. Left to our own devices, we would be trapped forever, not by anything outside of us, but by the encircling wall of our own belief. Therefore, the major force in our return to Heaven is what has traditionally been called "grace": divine assistance. We cannot make it alone, but we do not need to. In fact, all we need do is give the Holy Spirit a "little willingness"[23] and He will carry us the rest of the way.

To meet us where we are, the Holy Spirit translates the fundamental truth that Heaven is real and the world is not, into forms we can practically apply. His entire mission is perfectly designed to work within our present limitations in order to undo them. He realizes we cannot awaken from the world instantly, and so, He leads us home gradually, step by step, on a "…journey without distance to a goal that has never changed."[24] He guides us along what for most of us will be a very long road, from darkness to increasingly brilliant shades of light.

Along these same lines, the Holy Spirit does not ask us to overlook the world, but simply to see it differently. Therefore, the goal He holds out to us is not our ultimate goal, Heaven, but an interim one, the perception of what the Course calls the **real world,** the reflection of Heaven in the world. This is not only a more realistic, comprehensible goal, but it turns our energies away from the pitfall of withdrawing from the world in pursuit of Heaven. Seeing the real world means using our mind to look past the bodies that our eyes perceive, to something eternally valid within them, a pristine innocence, a holiness, a divinity within everyone. Each thing becomes a window onto a whole new world, an inner world, composed of the light of Heaven within everything.

To attain this shift in perception the Holy Spirit must loosen the control the outer world seems to have on our minds. He therefore translates into understandable, everyday terms the central idea that the world is our own dream. He emphasizes, not so much that we made the world, but that we create our *experience* within the world. The outside world does not control us; we are not its victims. Bodies, objects and events, being illusions, are completely neutral. They are empty forms and, like a Rorschach inkblot, can be seen however we choose. It is our own perception, our own interpretation of them that gives rise to our experience of life. And this perception is an internal matter. It is our own free choice.

The entire focus of the Holy Spirit, then, is on our perception, our thinking. The only meaningful choice we have is not between the forms outside of us but between different ways of thinking. And, according to the Holy Spirit, there are only two. These two mentalities are His translation of the basic distinction between truth and illusion into a form we can use within the illusion. One, called **wrong-mindedness,** is based on fear and chains us to the world. The other, **right-mindedness,** is based on love and reveals to us the real world.

Life under the Course's teaching, then, is supremely simple.

It is not enmeshed in the battle with the world, lamenting the past, worrying about the future, agonizing over the manipulation of forms. We make, over and over again, the one simple choice between love and fear. To make this choice, though, we must first understand it, and so we will now examine these two mindsets in greater depth.

WRONG-MINDEDNESS: THE EGO

Wrong-mindedness is a comprehensive thought-system that includes within it its own perception of the world, other people, God, everything. But this thought-system is anchored in a particular image of ourselves. The Course calls this image the **ego**. The ego, very simply, is our deeply ingrained belief that we are a separate self. It is the natural and obvious picture of the self we seem to be in this world. Housed within our own personal body is our own private mind to which we alone have direct access. We seem to think and feel, will and experience, suffer and find happiness, independently of anyone else.

Being a separate self may seem harmless enough, yet as soon as we believe we are separate we are inevitably drawn into a destructive relationship with the world around us. The reason is simple. If we are separate, what we gain, the world loses; what it has, we do not. The ego thus very quickly becomes an image of attack on the whole for the sake of ourselves. To eat, to be safe, to succeed, to survive at all, it appears that we must be the victor over our surroundings. This thought permeates us so deeply and so completely that it seems to be the essence of life itself, both human and natural; the maintenance and benefit of the individual based on the devouring and conquering of the world around it.

This pattern is the central dynamic of the ego and is what has traditionally been called **sin**. Sin is the violating of someone or something else for our own benefit. It is the individual will pitted against everything outside of it, waging war upon God and upon the world, breaking law, denying truth and violating reality.

What exactly is the goal of all this furious activity? The goal, and in fact the central purpose of the ego, is the building, the maintenance and the protection of the ego itself. Because we think the ego is what we are, we spend all of our time taking care of this image, carefully sculpting an ego that will give us self-worth and worth in the eyes of others, an ego that we hope can be loved. This is the commodity for which we compete against the world. We seek to wrest from the world and possess for ourselves the precious currency of love. We seek to be a "special" ego, a unique ego; one that is not only set apart, as are all egos, but is also set above, attracting to itself the priceless treasures of pride, power, adulation and love.

Under the goal of **specialness** and the means of sin, we relate to the world in two major ways. One is **attack**. Attack is the direct and natural expression of sin, in which we seek to overpower another, and from the defeat of his ego feed the specialness of our own. At root, attack is a mental act, the essence of which, ironically, is to *see sin in others;* to condemn, to be angry, to resent. Attack seeks to bring love to us, but is itself the direct opposite of love. "It is the judgment of one mind by another as unworthy of love and deserving of punishment."[25]

Direct attack, however, is a painful way of life, leaving us guilty, alone and encircled by enemies. We, therefore, set about seeking allies who can support our cause, ensure our safety, and feed our need for what we think is love. However, to obtain these allies, we must hide our real motives and sacrifice some of our interests. We must play their game while trying to win at our own. This is the second way we relate to the world, through **bargaining**, or **giving to get**. Here our apparent love may seem to be directed at the other person, but actually it is a boomerang, a baited hook, whose real trajectory lands it back at our own feet. Relationships based primarily on giving to get are called **special love relationships**, in which the two members strike a bargain, an implicit agreement that "love" will be mutually given on the condition that it is mutually returned. Whereas these relationships may seem opposite to **special hate relationships**, those based on attack, they are actually ruled by the identical strategy of using others to inflate our own specialness. The attack is subtle, but not absent.

Attack and giving to get have the selfsame purpose of collecting to ourselves what the Course calls **idols**. Idols are all those things we surround ourselves with to prove how special we are: money, possessions, achievements, abilities, beautiful bodies (our own and others'), vanquished enemies and prestigious friends. Idols seem to be what life is all about, and the more special are the idols which we possess and the more spacious and glittering is our entire collection, the more we seem to have fulfilled the essence of life itself.

It does not take penetrating insight to see that most of us spend most of our time in the ego's way of life. It is also quite obvious that it is not a very uplifting sight when looked at clearly. It is, in fact, grotesque, and this is the problem with the ego. Somewhere in our minds we are always looking at it clearly. Even though consciously we establish our identity through how the world sees and treats us, subconsciously our eyes are riveted on how we see and treat the world, as the true commentary on what we are.

The strategy of sin, then, produces massive **guilt** inside of us. If we sin, we deserve to be punished. If we condemn, we deserve to be condemned. Guilt is our self-punishment, our self-condemnation. Therefore, sin, which was designed to create self-worth, brings instead self-loathing. It seems to be an abysmal failure.

Yet, completely undaunted, the ego feels supported and strengthened by guilt. Guilt tells us that the ego is real, that its sinful picture of us is what we really are. We now have no one to turn to but our ego and no recourse but to run from our guilt. Defense mechanisms are the means for our escape. Their purpose is the straightforward one of simply throwing guilt, for the moment, out of sight.

The Course focuses on two defenses, **denial** and **projection,** which go hand in hand. Whereas denial hides guilt inside, projection throws it outside. Denial is the very simple act of suppressing our guilt, pushing it out of awareness into our subconscious. Projection, on the other hand, reinterprets our guilt, telling us that what seems to be our guilt is actually someone else's. In short, it blames others in order to escape blame ourselves. Projection fills our field of vision with guilt, blaming others, the world, God, anything but ourselves, for the sins we secretly believe to be our own.

Obviously, projection has no power to heal guilt. The sad truth is that this supposed escape from guilt actually causes guilt, setting in motion a whole cycle of guilt. This is because projection is just another form of attack, for the essence of both is to accuse others of sin. All that projection does is add another dimension to the same ego dynamics. Before, we used attack to steal "self-worth" from others. Now, we use projection to dump onto others negative self-worth (guilt). Whereas before we were the aggressive victimizer, now we are the weak, defensive victim. We visibly nurse our wounds, sending to the world the accusing message, "Behold me, brother, at your hand I die."[26] But, whether predator or prey, it is clearly the same attempt to save ourselves by damning others.

This entire system simply does not work. It, in fact, inevitably leads to the state of fear that the Course describes as the essence of the human condition. Having accused ourselves and others of sin, we have no alternative but to shrink into isolation and hide from the punishment of the evil without and the guilt within. This is the end result of the ego: fear, isolation, guilt, loneliness.

We now are in a position to grasp the essence of the ego more firmly. Earlier we said the ego is an attack on the whole for the sake of ourselves. In this the Course echoes many of the world's great spiritual traditions in identifying our core problem as what we call the "self" and its "selfishness." The Course, however, prefers the word "ego" and does not often use the word "selfishness" in describing it. It has a reason for this. The ego is not *really* an attack on the whole for the sake of ourselves. That is a lie told by the ego. It is an attack on everything, *including* ourselves. No one benefits from the ego, ourselves least of all. It destroys all as one. It is only an idea, but one that is nursed, pampered and brooded over at the expense of our own happiness and peace, and that of everyone around us. It is a parasite and we are its host.

That the ego is an attack on ourselves is obvious. By saying we are apart from and at war with the rest of reality, the ego accuses us of being small and alone, sinful and evil. It is a damning image, one that, if true, makes us deserving of the unhappiness we experience and the eternal punishment we have been told about.

Fortunately, the Course says the ego is not what we are. This is another way of phrasing the Course's core distinction between the reality of Heaven and the illusory world. We are not egos. We are not separate and we are not sinful. We are still as God created us: pure, innocent and infinite.

Even within this world the ego is an illusion. The mind which seems to be trapped in time and space is actually a portion of the Christ Mind and, therefore, cannot truly violate the laws of Heaven. What this means is that we are by nature incapable of the very cornerstone of the ego: sin. Sin is a mask, a disguise. Sin says that we gain pleasure from hurting others. Yet, in truth, hurting another hurts us, tormenting us with guilt. It therefore cannot be our real goal. It is, in our minds, a means, a necessary evil, a guilty way of attaining our real goal. Our real goal is the only thing we want, the only thing we *can* want: love. We saw earlier that this was the single goal of the entire machinery of the ego. No matter how cruel and ruthless we seem, we are really just seeking love, in the form of self-worth, seeking to be loved by others and by ourselves. What looks like sin, therefore, is a **call for love**. It is not the strong, confident, fully aware expression of what we are. Sin is really just a mistake: an attempt that does not succeed. It is a blind, frightened, desperate appeal for love.

Sin, therefore, is an illusion. It is something we are psychologically incapable of performing. It has literally never happened. We are not evil creatures deserving of guilt and torment. We may seem fearsome, but we are merely afraid. In truth, we are innocent children of God, who are not fallen and who are not evil, but are simply mistaken.

FORGIVENESS: RIGHT-MINDEDNESS

Forgiveness is the cornerstone of right-mindedness, and is the central teaching of *A Course in Miracles*. It is the perfect practical embodiment of the core lesson that fear is an illusion and only love is real. It is, therefore, the perfect transition from this world to Heaven. Locked in the dynamic of forgiveness is the power to heal our minds, to dispel our pain, and ultimately to awaken us from the confines of time and space.

By choosing forgiveness as its primary focus, the Course is making several very important statements. First, it is saying that the fundamental human problem is the pain which comes from sin: the guilt and fear of punishment. Forgiveness, of course, is the traditional remedy for the effects of sin, releasing the sinner from his debt of punishment and guilt. Second, the Course is saying that its goal is love, for the aim of forgiveness is the restoration of love. Forgiveness in effect says, "I will forget your sin and will instead love you." Third, by emphasizing forgiveness instead of love, the Course is saying that the problem of sin must be undone before the goal of love can be achieved. No matter how much energy we pour into trying to love ourselves or others, we will never succeed until we erase from our vision the dark cloud of sin.

The Course, however, says that forgiveness as normally understood cannot relieve the effects of sin and cannot achieve the goal of love. Normal forgiveness is based on the belief that sin is real, and if sin is real, then guilt is valid, punishment is just and forgiveness is a lie. Forgiveness thus becomes "...a vain attempt to look past what is there; to overlook the truth..."[27] Furthermore, if we are undeserving of forgiveness, then we cannot give it to ourselves. We can only beg for it. We can only hope and pray that the party we have injured, either another person or God Himself, will condescend to grant us the unmerited gift of forgiveness.

The Course's position is radically different. Sin, it says, is an illusion. Sin does not create a debt we must pay and does not need to be pardoned by an outside force. It is only a dream we must awaken from. The problem is only in our mind, and it is there it must be resolved. Therefore, the Course says, "Ask not to be forgiven, for this has already been accomplished. Ask, rather, to learn how to forgive...."[28] Nothing outside of us needs to change to make forgiveness possible. Forgiveness is the choice of our own mind to awaken from the belief in sin and have that replaced by the experience of love.

Although the Course urges us to forgive both ourselves and others, its main focus is on the forgiving of others. Why is this? The answer is to be found in the nature of the ego. The essence of the ego, if we recall, is in an antagonistic relationship with all of reality, with God, others and even ourselves; a thought of separateness from the whole and attack on the whole. The undoing of the ego is therefore the restoration of our mind's broken relationship with reality, a reuniting with ourselves, others and God. In this mental process of reunion it is other people who are our most immediate and potent representatives of the whole. God is too abstract. Our true feelings toward Him, both our infinite love and our titanic fear, are buried much too deeply. We ourselves are not appropriate representatives of the whole, for the ego has so profoundly convinced us that we are separate, that we gain from the loss of others. It is other people who become our best symbols of the whole we have rejected. It is in relation to them that our mind can best work out its severed relationship with totality. For it is in relation to them that the ego shows its true colors: attacking, rejecting, resenting; making manifest the ugliness that it really is. Furthermore, it is in relation to them that we can completely transcend the ego by reaching past separate boundaries and establishing a true joining, characterized by genuine love and giving. Therefore, in how we see other people we can both get in touch with our ego and get outside of our ego.

Forgiveness of others is indeed the single greatest challenge to the ego. Our ego is usually undisturbed by our weak attempts to love God and to feel self-worth, but is rocked to the core by a true relinquishment of the entrenched condemnation and fear that keep us separate from another human being. No matter how difficult and against our best interests it may seem, forgiveness of others is the key to clearing away the twisted, malignant citadel the ego has built inside of us.

Forgiveness goes well beyond the pardoning of specific offenses. It is, in principle, a deep-seated transformation of our entire defensive, suspicious and uncaring posture toward another. And by healing our relationship with one we transform our relationship with everything. Instead of constantly taking, of being a black hole that drains the lifeblood of the universe, we become a radiant point of giving. We come out of the closed, depressed stance of fear, and enter into the openness and oneness of love.

The Course, then, is identifying our belief in the sinfulness and evil in other people as the key element in the dream. It is this that locks in place the separateness and suffering that characterize the world. If we can just realize that the sin we see is an illusion, if we can pull this single lever, this invisible trigger, then we will overturn the entire basis for this world, and it will all begin to change. The light of Heaven will start to shine on our minds and on the world as well.

How do we forgive? Forgiveness follows a three-step healing process, of which the first two steps are ours and the last is left completely to the Holy Spirit.

STEP ONE is *identifying the problem*. Essentially, what this means is taking a clear, honest look at what we believe about another. This is quite a challenge, since the ego has tried to hide its darkness, using denial and projection to place itself beyond the realm of choice and change. Therefore we must reverse denial and bring to full awareness the condemning thoughts we hide. The Course often urges us to "search your mind for...unloving thoughts,"[29] for, "it is so crucial that you look upon your hatred and realize its full extent."[30] We must also reverse projection and understand that the sin we see in others is not necessarily their reality, but is simply our own mental creation, our own dream.

Now that we have our hands on the nuts and bolts of our ego, we are in a position to evaluate them. No matter how frightening this step may be, if we can stand back in calm detachment it will not be difficult to realize what we have discussed already: that the perception of sin in another is both untrue and unsatisfying. Our condemnation is neither a true expression of us nor a true reflection of our brother. What we thought was the sin of an evil mind was merely the cry for love of a son of God. Furthermore, our illusion brings us no reward. In the end, it only causes us pain, the pain of being a guilty ego alone in a fearful world.

STEP TWO is *letting go of the problem.* This is the step of forgiveness. The key to forgiving another is not to fight against our anger and seek to tear its "evil" from the living tissue of our heart. The key is to realize that the sin we see in the other is an illusion, a dream that hurts us, a laughable mistake. There is no reason whatsoever to hang onto our hatred, no reason to express it or suppress it. We can simply let it go.

This is forgiveness. We empty our minds of all the darkness we see in another and all our limiting judgments of what he is. We wipe the slate clean. And now we can reach out to a light in him that is not of this world, to a breath of God in him. We ask to be shown something inside him beyond the sight of our eyes and the grasp of our ego, something that can awaken our primordial sense of love and oneness and our innate desire to give. Forgiveness, therefore, is the relinquishing of the illusion of sin and is simultaneously "an earthly form of love,"[31] which carries within it the wish to be joined and the impulse to give.

STEP THREE *is the healing.* Forgiveness is an implicit prayer for the healing of our mind's sick picture of another person. This ushers in the power of the Holy Spirit, Who transforms our mental structures and infuses us with the gift of love. Now we can truly love this person. This profound change reverberates throughout the height and breadth of our belief system and causes a general shift in our entire outlook on life. We step increasingly into right-mindedness and find a happiness and peace we thought we could never know.

The Holy Spirit also brings healing to the other person. All of his pain came from the sad belief that he was an unworthy sinner. Now he sees in our eyes a new image of himself, one that is washed clean of guilt and filled with the light of God. He may not experience healing instantly, but on some level of his mind there is more light, waiting for the day when it will be accepted.

By healing our relationship with the whole, forgiveness also heals our own self-image. Just as our attack on others proved we were guilty, so our gift to another shows that there must be something good in us. In other words, we find a true sense of self-worth. "The perception of self-value come[s] from the extension of loving thoughts outward."[32] Also, by joining with another we dissolve the very nature of the ego. We prove that we are not alone and separate; we are not an ego.

The effects of forgiveness do not stop there. Because all minds are joined, any act of forgiveness rolls through the entire universe like a healing wave, lightening the load of all living things, bringing all minds closer to Heaven.

We now can see that forgiveness is the direct counterpoint to the ego, for the ego inflicts pain on everything within its grasp, shattering its world into fragmentation. Forgiveness, on the other hand, brings happiness and peace to all minds, uniting all under the healing umbrella of love. The ego looks outward to a dangerous world and inward to a guilty self, pulling us into the lonely, contracted whirlpool of fear. Forgiveness, again, does the exact opposite, showing us the light of God within everyone and releasing us into the outflowing, joyous union of love. Furthermore, the ego's system of fear is an illusion. Love alone is real. This is what makes possible the Course's central prescription, which is to let go of the illusion of fear, allowing it to be replaced by the reality of love.

Because genuine forgiveness is such a challenge to our ego, it usually does not come easy. The attainment of it involves deep-level transformations that for most of us seem to take a very long time. And yet the change of mind that forgiveness entails is the only thing that really works. It is the only answer that goes beyond superficial and temporary change, and brings true, lasting happiness.

Forgiveness, therefore, is not an isolated, part-time activity. It is, according to the Course, our sole function while on earth, our purpose for being here. We are to become teachers of God, saviors of the world, who, through bringing forgiveness to everyone, find forgiveness for ourselves. Through this process we both teach and learn that we are all one, not separate; that none of us makes it back until we all do. Therefore, we devote all of our efforts to seeing and making manifest the real world, the reflection of Heaven on earth, from which we all return home together.

Forgiveness is the perfect application of the Course's central distinction between the reality of Heaven and the illusory world. It shows us, in practical ways, in the heart of our daily lives, that all the obstacles we see to Heaven are simply the hallucination of our own minds. For, by simply changing our minds, by forgiving, we come to see a part of Heaven in everyone and everything we look upon. Thus, it is through forgiveness that we will return to Heaven. One day, in the distant future, the very fabric of time and space will unravel, the world will vanish, and we will be back in Heaven, with our Father, again.

QUOTATIONS FROM

A Course in Miracles

The language of the Course is a study in itself, possessing a rare combination of power, poetry, grandeur and grace. Lacking all timidness and careless of a need to qualify its statements, it achieves a sweeping force of vividness and impact. Even though it bypasses traditional "thee's" and "thou's" and uses contemporary language, it creates a feeling of majesty and holiness, even in the midst of theoretical discussions. The Course is also filled with great beauty, and even contains actual poetry, in that much of it, including most of the Workbook for Students, is written in an exacting form of poetic verse called iambic pentameter, a form used and developed by Shakespeare.

The following are selected quotations which communicate the style and content of *A Course in Miracles.*

*   *   *

The holiest of all the spots on earth is where an ancient hatred has become a present love.[33]

The Holy Spirit's temple is not a body, but a relationship.[34]

When you meet anyone, remember it is a holy encounter.
As you see him you will see yourself.
As you treat him you will treat yourself.
As you think of him you will think of yourself.
Never forget this, for in him you will find yourself or lose yourself.[35]

Everything you teach you are learning.
Teach only love, and learn that love is yours and you are love.[36]

It is impossible to remember God in secret and alone...The lonely journey fails because it has excluded what it would find.[37]

When a brother behaves insanely, you can heal him only by perceiving the sanity in him.[38]

It is impossible to overestimate your brother's value.[39]

Having *rests on giving and not on getting.*[40]

To have, give all to all.[41]

Seek not to change the world, but choose to change your mind about the world.[42]

When any situation arises which tempts you to become disturbed...say: "There is another way of looking at this."[43]

In every difficulty, all distress,
and each perplexity Christ calls to you
and gently says, "My brother, choose again."[44]

Now you must learn that only infinite patience produces immediate effects.[45]

Health is the result of relinquishing all attempts to use the body lovelessly.[46]

You must have noticed an outstanding characteristic of every end that the ego has accepted as its own. When you have achieved it, it has not satisfied you.[47]

You think you hold against your brother what he has done to you. But what you really blame him for is what you *did to* him.[48]

All anger is nothing more than an attempt to make someone feel guilty...[49]

Beware of the temptation to perceive yourself unfairly treated.[50]

All your past except its beauty is gone, and nothing is left but a blessing.[51]

A miracle is never lost. It may touch many people you have not even met, and produce undreamed of changes in situations of which you are not even aware."[52]

The journey to God is merely the reawakening of the knowledge of where you are always, and what you are forever. It is a journey without distance to a goal that has never changed.[53]

Heaven itself is reached with empty hands and open minds, which come with nothing to find everything and claim it as their own.[54]

The Holy Spirit's Voice is as loud as your willingness to listen.[55]

You can refuse to enter, but you cannot bar the door that Christ holds open. Come unto me who holds it open for you, for while I live it cannot be shut, and I live forever.[56]

"I am here only to be truly helpful.
I am here to represent Him Who sent me.
I do not have to worry about what to say or what to do, because He Who sent me will direct me.
I am content to be wherever He wishes, knowing He goes there with me.
I will be healed as I let Him teach me to heal."[57]

A Course in Miracles

Q. Is *A Course in Miracles* a class that is taught?

A. A Course in Miracles is a self-study book, designed for individual application of its principles. Many people, however, have found it helpful to study the Course in groups as a way of better understanding the material. Although some people have felt led to teach its concepts, there is no authorization program for teachers.

Q. Is the Course affiliated with any church or religion?

A. No. The Course is simply a set of books. It is not a publication of any religion or denomination. The Foundation for Inner Peace, a nonprofit organization, is the copyright holder whose sole purpose is to publish the material as originally specified by the author.

Q. Which of the three volumes should be read first?

A. One can begin study of the Course with any of the three Volumes.[58] While the Text and Workbook for Students are not structured to be done concurrently, they clearly complement each other. All the volumes combine to produce a whole system, meaning that full study of the Course requires use of each volume at some point in time.

Q. Is complete mastery of each lesson in the Workbook for Students necessary before going on to the next?

A. "Learning will not be hampered when you miss a practice period because it is impossible at the appointed time...But learning will be hampered when you skip a practice period because you are unwilling to devote the time..."[59] Many have found help in taking more than one day for a lesson, yet perfection is not required, since complete mastery of any one lesson would mean that no further lessons would be needed. All that the Course requires is that not more than one lesson be done on a particular day.

Q. Is a student finished with the Course upon completing the Workbook for Students?

A. "This course is a beginning, not an end."[60] This quotation is found at the end of the Workbook, an indication that *A Course in Miracles* sees its course of learning as a lifelong process. The Course is meant for deep study and most students find that progress is slow, but certain. Some students are guided to go through the Workbook several times, while others may complete it just once. In either case the principles of the Course are intended to be continually applied throughout one's life.

Q. Why does the Course use only masculine gender?

A. The Course always seeks to simplify the complexities of the world and the differences that lie between people. Therefore it simply ignores differences of sex and exclusively utilizes masculine pronouns, traditionally the preferred usage in English literature and in Christianity. Some people have difficulty with this and have found it helpful to mentally substitute the words "child," "daughter" and "sister" for the Course's "son" and "brother."

Q. When the Course says that forgiveness shows us the light in another, what does it mean?

A. Seeing light in another is a mental sensing of holiness within them. It is not at all seeing a visual light, for instance a light around another's body. However, such an experience may occur as a symbol of perceiving the true light within them.

Q. How does one know when he has forgiven someone completely?

A. Forgiveness is a lengthy process of which there are many degrees of achievement. When we are truly able to forgive any one person completely, we have reached the level of someone such as Jesus and can totally forgive everyone.

Q. What place does the practice of meditation have in the Course?

A. Meditation is an example of the Course's emphasis on letting go of our ego-based thoughts and leaving an empty space through which the Holy Spirit can enter into our minds. As such, it plays an important part in the Workbook, which contains specific instructions for meditation in lessons 41, 44, 45, 47, 49, 69, 70, 94, 109, 125, 131, 164, 183, 188, 189.

Q. Based on the Course, how does one know what to do in specific situations, and which stands to take on particular issues?

A. The Course takes no stands on specific issues and sets forth no code of behavior. Since behavior is a symbol of our thoughts we must always concentrate first on the healing of our thoughts. Only then can we deal with the important issue of how to express that intent in the form of words, behavior or an opinion. In this decision we are then to turn to the Holy Spirit for guidance.

Q. In receiving guidance from the Holy Spirit, how does one hear His Voice and distinguish it from the ego's?

A. The main purpose of the Holy Spirit is as a healer of our thoughts, mostly on the unconscious level. We can, however, receive specific guidance from Him. The essential qualities for this are desire, willingness and receptivity. Guidance seems to come in many forms and requires careful discernment to separate the pure from the impure. For deciding if an idea is of the Holy Spirit, the Course suggests the following test: Does its application inspire peace in ourselves and others, despite the fact that on the surface it may be threatening to the ego?

Q. How does the Course view the use of medicine?

A. Although the Course asserts that medicine cannot truly heal anything, since the body is an illusion and the true problem is within, it does say that it is acceptable to turn to medicine for temporary relief when we are unable to accept healing for our body through the healing of our mind.

Q. Is the purpose of the Course's principles the acquisition of material gain?

A. No. The Course says that the physical world is illusory and that attachment to the things of the world is solely a characteristic of the ego. There is a purpose for material things but only as instruments to aid us in our function as bringers of forgiveness to the world.

Q. According to the Course, why did we originally separate from God?

A. "The ego will demand many answers that this Course does not give."[61] There are a few reasons why the Course will not answer this question. First, it says that in reality we have never separated.[62] Second, to give a reason why the separation even seemed to occur would endow it with the attributes of reality; would make it seem reasonable and therefore more justified in continuing. Third, the Course seeks to focus our attention always on the present, away from the past, for it is only in the present that we can stop repeating the choice to separate and make a different choice.[63]

Q. Was additional material received by Helen Schucman that is not found in the Course?

A. Following the completion of the Course, additional material was taken down by Helen and later published in two pamphlets entitled *Psychotherapy: Purpose, Process and Practice* and *The Song of Prayer*. These writings serve as excellent extensions and summaries of the Course's principles. A collection of Helen's inspired poetry, *The Gifts of God*, was published in 1982.

Q. What has happened to the original participants in the story of the Course?

A. Helen Schucman died in February, 1981. Bill Thetford retired from Columbia University in 1978 and continued to study the Course with friends until his death in July, 1988. Judy Skutch is president of the Foundation for Inner Peace, and is working closely with the process of translating the Course into other languages. Ken Wapnick is a writer and teaches Course theory at the Foundation for A Course in Miracles, which he founded with his wife, Gloria.

THE IMPACT OF
A Course in Miracles

It is clear that *A Course in Miracles* is not meant for everyone. It itself affirms that the Holy Spirit works to meet the specific and highly individual needs of each person and that "There is a course for every teacher of God."[64] Yet it is equally clear that the Course has come into the world for a purpose and that there are many whose needs are being met by it. In fact, since its publication in 1976, the Course's circle of friends has been widening at an almost explosive rate. Its history after publication has been as phenomenal as its history prior to publication and as unique as is the Course itself.

Curiously enough, the Course has something to offend almost everyone. As much as any teaching in existence it seems to throw caution utterly to the wind. For a secular age, it is too spiritual. For those into alternative spirituality, it is too Christian. For Christians, it is too Eastern. For those into self-help, it is too emphatic about helping others and being helped by God. And for all of us, it presents deep, seemingly insurmountable challenges to our ego.

For these reasons, primarily the latter, there are many stories of people in fits throwing their books away, flushing them down toilets, throwing them in rivers, etc. Yet these very acts highlight one of the most interesting phenomena surrounding the Course: The tremendous power it has over people, its dynamic appeal. For who would be that angry with the Course unless they were taking it very seriously?

A Course in Miracles seems to have the ability to reach deep inside people's hearts and minds and establish an inner dialogue with them, calling them on the games they play, bringing to light their secret shames, leading them to question the assumptions their life is built on, to reconsider their feelings toward others and to entertain the possibility of the eternally good. Almost immediately the Course is treated like family, both moving people and angering them; being at once loved, hated and wrestled with.

The appeal of the Course is seemingly universal and cuts across all social, cultural and religious boundaries. Possessing an amazing ability for winning over the most unlikely friends and bringing together people of the most diverse backgrounds, the Course has been adopted by Jews, Protestants, Catholics, people involved in "New Age" type groups, agnostics and atheists; by ministers, psychologists, business people, teachers, artists and politicians; by adults of all ages and by people of many, many nationalities.

People respond so deeply to the Course that many of them are won over heart and soul and devote their lives to it. Some teach it or write books based on it. Others establish Course-based organizations. Many just study it at home, perhaps with some friends, and begin the quiet, life-long process of becoming a living example of its principles.

What is the source of the Course's appeal? Aside from its very evident ability to transform people and heal relationships, there is something else. There emerges from its symphony of words and ideas, of system, style and artistry, a distinct feeling, like an overtone hovering above the music. It is this feeling, in addition to and beyond the actual content of what is said, that is much of the drawing power of the material. Helen Schucman, scribe of the Course, put her finger on the nature of this quality:

> *Nor did I understand the calm but impressive authority with which the Voice dictated. It was largely because of the strangely compelling nature of this authority that I refer to the Voice with a capital "V ." I do not understand the real authorship of the writing, but the particular combination of certainty, wisdom, gentleness, clarity and patience that characterized the Voice makes that form of reference seem perfectly appropriate.*[65]

This "combination of certainty, wisdom gentleness, clarity and patience" is the force that drew Helen back, again and again, to the process of dictation, and is the same force that draws students to the Course today from all over the world. What is it? It is clearly nothing other than the personality of the author shining through the pages and print of these volumes. Although it does not parade the fact, nor demand acceptance of it, the Course's claim is obvious: that the author of the material is Jesus Christ. This idea, though startling, can give us some basis for understanding the phenomenon of *A Course in Miracles*. For both the Jesus of history and the Jesus of the Course demonstrate that same mysterious, compelling magnetism, calling forth a wave of inspiration, devotion and love throughout masses of men and women.

The Course's wave, though comparatively small at this time, is spreading with a life, a spontaneity and a rapidity that is somewhat reminiscent of the tidal wave that was unleashed some 2000 years ago at the death of Jesus of Nazareth. Its influence is presently washing into every sector of society, so that one might hear it quoted at a business seminar, a "New Age" event, or a psychological convention, in a Catholic seminary or from a Protestant pulpit. Besides having more than one million copies in print itself, the Course has inspired dozens of books based on it, some of them actually outselling the Course, such as Gerald Jampolsky's best-selling *Love is Letting Go of Fear* and Marianne Williamson's *A Return to Love*. Thousands of small groups that meet to study the material have arisen spontaneously in homes and churches across the country and around the world. In addition to this, several spiritual organizations and retreat centers have been founded, dedicated either primarily or solely to the teachings of the Course. Furthermore, the Course is currently being translated into over a dozen languages, among which are French, German, Spanish, Italian, Hebrew and Russian.

All of this is rather remarkable considering the fact that there is no worldly machinery powering this wave. It has no central organization pouring resources into it. There is no paid advertising for the Course (one of the original stipulations of the Voice). And there is no external personality, no figurehead to fire people's emotions and whip them into a movement. The only power behind this movement is the power of the Course itself, its magnetism and its ability to directly touch people's lives and heal them.

And yet there is more. For behind the scenes of all this wild activity, the unseen presence of the author appears to still be at work, just as he was in the early years that led up to the Course's publication. The plan that produced the Course seems still to be going forward, in a dance full of unexpected turns, just as in the beginning when Helen and Bill never knew what was coming next. People are still being called upon and raised up to do their part. The Course is daily finding itself in new pairs of hands through highly coincidental and seemingly carefully arranged series of events. It is still fulfilling the same kind of spiritual searches and answering the same kind of desperate prayers that were offered up by the Course's original participants.

If the plan is still going on, the question arises, where will it end? The Course seems to have come into the world for a purpose, to fulfill a mission. As Helen was told by the Voice, in material not included in the books:

> *The world situation is worsening to an alarming degree. People all over the world are being called on to help, and are making their individual contributions as part of an overall prearranged plan. Part of the plan is taking down* A Course in Miracles, *and I am fulfilling my part in the agreement, as you will fulfill yours.* [66]

If the Course is here for a purpose, one must wonder what its ultimate destiny is to be. What is the final significance of *A Course in Miracles* for the world? Again we may be able to get some handle on this by returning to the issue of authorship. If we grant for the moment that Jesus really is the author of the Course and if we also grant the Course's claim that Jesus is the leader in the "overall prearranged plan" to save the world, then it looks as if the central figure in history and the spiritual shepherd of mankind has arranged an extended, detailed communication, handing down to us in a whirl of miraculous events, a 1200 page book as an answer to our deepest, innermost problem. This book is clearly intended as a kind of large-scale correction for the errors in mankind's spiritual systems, especially in the religion founded by Jesus himself. And this book seems to have been transmitted through its human scribe with crystal clarity, even to the point of enabling the author to communicate in an exacting form of poetic verse.

Pondering the implications of these ideas and taking into consideration all that has been said about this remarkable, utterly unique phenomenon called *A Course in Miracles*, our visions of the Course's future can become very broad indeed. One cannot help but get the feeling that we have possibly witnessed the birth of a new star in the sky of human history, one whose brilliance may in the end lead millions of people along the path of love and may eventually shape the patterns of global civilization. But whatever the exact form of its ultimate destiny, it will almost certainly be just as unexpected as was that first night, when out of the blue Helen heard a Voice saying, "This is *A Course in Miracles*. Please take notes."

NOTES

T = *A Course in Miracles: Text.* Mill Valley, Calif: Foundation for Inner Peace, 1975.

W = *A Course in Miracles: Workbook for Students.* Mill Valley, Calif: Foundation for Inner Peace, 1975.

M = *A Course in Miracles: Manual for Teachers.* Mill Valley, Calif: Foundation for Inner Peace, 1975.

P = *Psychotherapy: Purpose, Process and Practice.* Mill Valley, Calif: Foundation for Inner Peace, 1975.

H = *A Course in Miracles: How It Came, What It Is, What It Says.* Mill Valley, Calif: Foundation for Inner Peace, 1975.

J = Skutch, Robert. *Journey Without Distance.* Berkeley, Calif: Celestial Arts, 1984.

1. W, 143
2. M, 71
3. T, 16
4. M, 3
5. M, 1
6. T, 499
7. W, 330
8. T, 52
9. M, 77
10. M, 65
11. T, 389
12. T, 362
13. P, 5f.
14. J, 51f.
15. T, introduction
16. H, 4
17. H, 4
18. J, 104
19. J, 119
20. T, 548
21. T, 542
22. W, 419

23. T, 380
24. T, 150
25. T, 236
26. T, 566
27. W, 248
28. T, 279
29. W, 51
30. T, 242
31. W, 353
32. T, 228
33. T, 562
34. T, 437
35. T, 142
36. T, 100
37. T, 295
38. T, 167
39. T, 434
40. T, 110
41. T, 106
42. T, 445
43. W, 50
44. T, 666

45. T, 88
46. T, 157
47. T, 155
48. T, 369
49. T, 319
50. T, 563
51. T, 83
52. T, 6
53. T, 150
54. W, 247
55. T, 157
56. T, 202
57. T, 28
58. M, 70
59. W, 201
60. W, 487
61. M, 77
62. M, 81
63. T, 56
64. M, 3
65. J, 134
66. J, 60

RESOURCES FOR
A Course in Miracles

HOW TO OBTAIN *A COURSE IN MIRACLES*

A Course in Miracles is available in hardcover and softcover editions as well as in audio and CD-ROM formats. Please visit our website at **www.miraclecenter.org** or call 1-800-359-ACIM(2246) or 714-632-9005 to order. You may also request a catalog by writing to the Miracle Distribution Center at the address shown on page 53 of this book.

MIRACLE DISTRIBUTION CENTER

Founded in 1978, Miracle Distribution Center is the only nonprofit organization of its kind that serves as a worldwide contact point for students of *A Course in Miracles.* The Center offers a full range of services associated with the Course including:

The Holy Encounter, a bimonthly publication of the Center has become, for many students of the Course, an invaluable tool for spiritual awareness and growth. Inspiring articles, in-depth interviews and information on *A Course in Miracles* around the world makes this an indispensable resource for anyone interested in the Course. There is no charge for the newsletter, but your kind donation will ensure that this important aspect of the Center's ministry continues to serve Course students across the globe.

MDC Online at "www.miraclecenter.org" offers most of the Center's valuable resources instantly on the Internet. Up-to-the-minute Course news and information, live real-time chat to connect with other Course students, thousands of study group listings, an extensive catalog of books and tapes, timely listings of Course events and much more can be found on our website.

U.S and International Study Group Listings are compiled and updated daily by Center staff. The world's most comprehensive and accurate database of *A Course in Miracles* study groups is made available by mail and on the Internet for Course students worldwide.

A Comprehensive Catalog of Course related books, audio and video tapes, CDs and more. If it relates to *A Course in Miracles*, the Center likely stocks it and will ship it out within 24 hours of your order.

Weekly Study Group Meetings to unlock the truths of *A Course in Miracles* every Wednesday evening at 7:00 p.m. facilitated by Beverly Hutchinson McNeff at the Center.

Study Group Tapes and CDs by mail are available every week. Even though the Course itself says it is simple, it is not necessarily always easy to understand and apply. It is for this reason we have been recording our study group meetings at the Center and sending them around the world. As a student of the Course since 1977 and president of the Center, Beverly provides insight into the Course that is penetrating and practical. Listeners experience a meditation, lecture and discussion about the Course that brings it alive. Each recording runs 80 minutes and is $6.50. Call the Center for details.

Miracle Prayer Ministry provides prayerful support with a designated prayer joining time of 4:30 (Pacific Time) each afternoon.

The Pen Pal Project helps Course students around the world find one another to correspond by mail or e-mail.

The Counseling Referral Service provides assistance for Course students seeking qualified counselors in their area who are sympathetic to the principles of *A Course in Miracles*.

The Lesson Phone Line presents an abridged recorded version of the daily lesson from the Course Workbook. Just dial (714) 7-SPIRIT.

Conferences, Seminars and Workshops bring together top Course teachers and students from all over the world. See *The Holy Encounter* or the Center's website for scheduled events.

HOW TO OBTAIN ADDITIONAL COPIES OF THIS BOOKLET

1 - 9 copies - $4.00 each
10 - 24 copies - $3.00 each
25 - 99 copies - $2.40 each
100 + copies - $1.80 each

Miracle Distribution Center
3947 East La Palma Avenue
Anaheim, California 92807
(714) 632-9005
Fax: (714) 632-9115
Website: www.miraclecenter.org
E-mail: info@miraclecenter.org